THE TREMOR OF RACEHORSES

The Tremor of Racehorses

SELECTED POEMS

SYLVA FISCHEROVÁ

TRANSLATED BY
JARMILA & IAN MILNER

BLOODAXE BOOKS

ISBN: 1 85224 106 3

First published 1990 by
Bloodaxe Books Ltd,
P.O. Box 1SN,
Newcastle upon Tyne NE99 1SN.

This book is published with the financial support
of the Arts Council of Great Britain.

Bloodaxe Books Ltd also acknowledges
the financial assistance of Northern Arts.

Typesetting by EMS Phototypesetting, Berwick upon Tweed.

Printed in Great Britain by
Billing & Sons Limited, Worcester.

Acknowledgements

These translations are of poems from the anthologies *Zvláštní znamení*/Special Sign (Československý Spisovatel, 1985) and *Klíčení: Almanach mladé české poezie*/ Germinating (Mladá Fronta, 1985), and from Sylva Fischerová's collections *Chvění závodních koní*/The Tremor of Racehorses (Mladá Fronta, 1986) and *Velká zrcadla*/Large Mirrors (Československý Spisovatel, 1990).

Acknowledgements are due to the editors of the following publications in which some of these translations first appeared: *Field* (Oberlin, USA), *New Edinburgh Review*, *Times Literary Supplement* and *Verse*. Some were included in the Child of Europe readings at the Royal Festival Hall, South Bank, London, in February 1989, published in the Child of Europe programme, and broadcast on BBC Radio 3.

Acknowledgements and thanks are also due to the Arts Council of Great Britain for providing a grant for Jarmila and Ian Milner to translate this selection of Sylva Fischerová's poems for Bloodaxe Books.

Contents

III

Introduction

Sylva Fischerová is a young poet, born in 1963. She has had two collections published and been well represented in two Czech anthologies. Her awareness of being a woman is expressed as a diffused natural sensibility that colours the texture of the poetry without insistence. At an early age she has found her own voice, alive with a gusty energy, capable of intimate personal exploration and sharp-eyed social observation. You hear it in many of her opening lines, which even in translation appeal by their rightness of touch and tone: 'I won't have regrets, I won't love. Too well/ combed leopards − ', 'I hear it all, I know/ it all, the quarrelsome voices', 'I saw my mother/ watering for the thousandth time/ a dead ibiscus', 'And why not, said Eve/ and the serpent smiled'.

Her voice, even when intimate, is no cry from the heart, no assertion of the ego. A self-distancing idiom gives the feeling an impersonal perspective. There is no blurring of the feminine viewpoint. Conventional masculine assumptions and approaches are ironicised with neat wit in poems like 'The Gate of My Private Cemetery but Without Leopards', 'Tiredness', 'Lovers in the Sand', 'We wanted to be silent'. Sometimes she writes love poems of relaxed tenderness or deep feeling: 'Black Tiger', 'Deep into the Body', '18/1/85', 'Go and Say a Prayer for Me, Sister', 'Jasmine Wind'.

Sylva Fischerová is unmistakably a poet of her Czech, more precisely Moravian, homeland, though distinct from any of her contemporaries, of whatever generation. Her flexible stylistic range, precision of word and image, and surrealist-tinged imagination distance her from the deep-rooted, often prolix and over-coloured Czech lyric tradition. Nor is she interested in the matter-of-fact procedures of the 'poetry of everyday' still prevalent, especially when such verse indulges in declaratory or moralising attitudes. As Czech critics have observed, Fischerová speaks for her generation − in the period before the recent democratic revolution − with a natural response such as Miroslav Holub and Josef Hanzlík, in different ways, received so strikingly from their early poetry in the 1960s.

Nowhere are her Czech roots more apparent than in her poems of social comment and protest. In his poetry translated in the 1960s, Holub became well-known internationally for his barbed and witty ironic exposures of authoritarian repression in post-1948 Communist Czechoslovakia. Sylva Fischerová has written effectively on this theme (e.g. poems like 'Drinking Coffee', 'Mechanisms', 'The Garden', 'Rowanberries', 'Irreversible Smiles'). But her eye has fixed on a special aspect of repression: the occupation of her country by the Soviet-led Warsaw Pact armed forces in 1968. Poems such as 'Necessary', 'Give Me Ashes, Earth and My Dead', 'The Merriest Country in the World' stand, and will stand, as classic expressions of that traumatic phase of Czechoslovak history. They have a strength of dramatic impact and a structural logic that one mightn't expect from the author so attached in other poems to fantasy and myth.

'No ideas but in things' said William Carlos Williams. Fischerová's poetic is often one of oblique rather than direct vision: she is more interested in what 'things' may become when transmuted or recreated by fancy and fantasy, sometimes extravagantly surreal. She is fascinated by metamorphosis sensed as a universal process underlying the human predicament of living and dying. It pervades poems like 'The Death Mask', 'And They Are Coming, the Guests Waiting for the Liquor', 'Making Tea', 'Girl with a Hasidic Candle' and others. Sometimes the shifts and abrupt dislocations in the poetic flow take you into the world of *Alice in Wonderland.*

Many of the poems in the concluding part of the book seek primarily to evoke the atmosphere of imagined experience. There is little or no pursuit of a poetic argument. The ambience of event is all. An instance is the beautifully phrased and shaped 'When They Return to Holy Troy', which opens:

> They will have everything:
> smiles and flowers and women,
>
> they will bring long afternoons
>   for the hands on the faces,
> when the unicorns in the eyes
>   raise
> their fearful horn
> in the green and white landscape
> and the small birds
> turn round and say, Yes?

Some readers may miss the 'sense of an ending' in these poems and feel that an initial promising potential of meaning has melted into thin air. Others will hear them for what they are: musical transcripts of the poetic imagination.

Another kind of poem emerges when Sylva Fischerová's keen

sense of 'things' blends with her imaginative insight, her awareness of mystery and metamorphosis at the heart of things. You find such a fusion in the moving poem 'The Pripet Marshes':

> I thought of you
> during my long train journey
> to where the world ends. Where the fields lie listless,
>   the flowers faded
>   in puked colours.
> Where the lungs are a cowshed, the land's
> only life. And the warm straw may catch fire
>   at any moment.
>
> The dead mirror of the marshes reflected for me
> a stranger's face; who was down there, who was burying
>   treasure under the bog?
>
> The reeds swayed and laughed
> and my hand kneaded
> the living mud, all the warm unburied
>   dead.
>
>   Above in the brown sky
>   hung a heavy bell
>   and its heart
>   beat out the hidden
>   deep under the bog
>   and sounded the measure of the Lord.

There is a different, more sombre music here. And at the close, though cryptic, an echo of what is heard in other poems: intimations of an unpredictable other-worldly Presence. That she writes such poems alongside the ironic "love" pieces, the controlled anger of the poems of protest, and the atmospheric fantasias, underlines the variety of her poetic vision and the quality of her craft.

IAN MILNER
Prague, March 1990

I

The Merriest Country in the World

He sat down and said:
    Play me the trumpet
        as if it were a flute,
    play me the double-bass
        as if it were a harp.

It was the best orchestra in the world.
    They played.

He said:
    Snap the strings
    and play a love song.

They snapped the strings
and the second violinist kissed
        the violin.

He said:
    Play the Apocalypse.

It was the best orchestra in the world.
    They put down their instruments
    and stood with empty
        hands.

He said:
    That is the first
    of the horsemen.
And before their eyes he burnt the violas,
violins, drumskins,
melted the trumpets and cymbals.
    That was the second, he said.

    And do you know
    which is the third?
    Under the rifle muzzles
    to play their anthem.

        And the fourth is
        to play it yourselves,

without compulsion,
interlace it
with snatches of Mozart
and think that you've saved
something.

It was the dress rehearsal
in case of occupation.

After the occupation
they summoned the best orchestra in the world
and said:
Play waltzes, polkas, gallopades,
gallopades, polkas, waltzes.

For ages now
it's been the merriest country in the world.

Am I My Brother's Keeper?

That was what he asked then
and there was a sudden heaviness upon earth like
>> when a bird spits
>> when a woman in bed turns her back
>>>> on a man.

We shall guard our brothers, you said
in that night of the valkyries, fires and songs from Valhalla.
But even then you knew you were lying.
Even then you knew your love
was scarcely more than
>> 'not to lose self-esteem'.
Even then you knew that you were too many
for Him to condemn all.

>> No one wanted that oath
>> from you. And the eyes of the valkyries
burn on in the darkness
>>> like gilded spittle
>>> like the Inquisition.

Necessary

What was necessary
   we did.

The fields lay fallow
   and we ploughed them,
   sowed the grain
      and waited.
Our women lay fallow
   and we did what was necessary
      and waited.

When foreign riders came
   we did what was necessary
   fenced off the fields and houses,
   sharpened axes and knives.

But at night the riders
      jumped the fences
      on their high horses
      and played the flute
      under our bedroom windows.
We put up higher and higher fences
but the horses grew
      as fast as the fences
      and the flute played on.

Then our women left us
   and took the children with them.
   We did what was necessary
   burnt the remnants of their dresses,
      the flowers behind the windows,
   and waited.

But no one has come.
      The stoves are cold,
      we go on waiting.

Maybe we've done less
                than was necessary?
                Or more?
And what if earlier,
before the riders came,
we had done less or more
and now we've done
                enough,
but that's why
we can't wait to see,
since only the one
who does less
                or more
reaches the end of waiting?

We don't know what to do
or whether to wait,
for by waiting
                we're doing something.
Or aren't we?
We don't know what's necessary.
                And the stoves are cold.

Give Me Ashes, Earth and My Dead

Give me ashes, earth and my dead.
    Deranged by a holiday the town
    swings a bit above ground,
    but will soon fall down. Then
Phoenix will fly in, and nibble the corpses
            and coat buttons
            and walls. But I did

warn you: it's a festive bird
          with gaudy feathers and colourful gob.
You reached out a hand
to others. You honoured the festivals.
You built towers.
And then you
shook hands together.

There's still time – to withdraw as far as possible into oneself,
          and take the ashes, earth and one's dead.

        The houses balance
        in a fearful equilibrium.

Drinking Coffee

I hear it all, I know
it all, the quarrelsome voices,

Nothing – Something – Everything –
and grab what you can, I know it,

you don't eat broth,
you drink broth, my foot stepping forward
                halts, I know it,

eyes and coffee and a raven
behind the window, tamed

ravens drinking coffee
and croaking KING KING, I know it

newts and Švejks and run away and play,
                fog is milk,
                good to drink,
my raised hand
halts, I know it,

broth and milk and coffee
for tamed ravens,
                tamed ravens
                without a king
                in Prague and fog,
                grab what you can.

Mechanisms

If you haven't
a fixed place to sleep, you'll understand,
                              otherwise you won't:
    the feeling that by pure chance
    after an evening party
    someone vomited you,
         threw you up: 'and that is
the last fence of mechanism,' said the anaemic painter
    who painted
    only red yellow white sheets –
         life's three primary colours. O those worn-out
channels of thought, those cement phrases from the newspapers:
the mechanism that it's more than
    a matter of mechanism, I
am no omniscient god, little fish on the pyramid of heaven,
supreme judge,
    laissez-moi vivre, you afternoon yellow winds
that whisper:
    We must eat and we must drink. That is
    all.
         You afternoon yellow winds that eat
my hair and drink my blood.

Completely New Times, a Completely New Age

For years
we would say to one another: between night and morning.

And later: between non-time
and time.

And we began
to make clocks, small
and large
and still larger,
until someone
built a house
inside the clocks,
his house,
and we built
clocks within clocks
and houses within houses,
houses in clocks
and clocks in houses,
so that no one knew
where he really lived
and the monster clocks
didn't show a thing

and everywhere
we looked for mirrors
when we were woken
by the quiet chimes,
but it could have been
marching

and we said to one another how wonderful
to be done with the small
first lie,
how heroic
to be consistent.

The Garden

I listen
to my steps resounding
from the walls of the darkened arbour,
with gleaming roses,
a weighty ornament, like the music of études
by young Mozarts
in white wigs.
It is lifeless here and dark. Those stray
shining leaves
falling like forgetting, white statues
with arms outstretched into emptiness
as if saying:
'emptiness can be touched,
it's cold and dry,
take some,
nothing dies
in this pastel darkness of mould
and extinction
is distant, further than our stretched arms
point to –

and so we've stayed here,
eyes glazed, white, toothless,
falling like forgetting,
laved by emptiness.'

And round and round
the resounding arbour
the ever monotonous
movements of feet
to the rhythm of tired études,
tired powdered
wigs that somewhere long ago rotted away –
Here nothing rots, decay
caresses everything with white stone hands, and the only sound
is my steps, as if
they were trying to get somewhere.

It swings
from side to side, but the sides of the ornament
are the same,
even the gesture of the statues
is always the same, the same whiteness
and the fractured greyness below the flower-beds,
stiffened entities, leaves strayed
to no purpose, my hands
laved by emptiness
to the rhythm of the études
weary as forgetting,
like the white changing of generations,
like time;

like my steps
in this Paradise,
in this imitation of Inferno,

the labyrinth of the ornament,
labyrinth of the ornament,
labyrinth of the ornament.

Irreversible Smiles

Irreversible smiles. The light that slides
round the shoulders of the statues

– what if they're not shoulders, in this sanctified
dance of certainties
any statement
is very risky –

and yet they are shoulders. Firm, you can
lean on them, when everyone
has left – statues in the bathroom, by the TV,
in front of the bed – so lifeless, so firm. When will the demolition
squad come?

I won't style anyone. Irreversible
smiles thrown at anybody
right in the eye, so he won't see, the nit-wit, smiling nit-wit.

Trouble is there's always something
to hand out. Smiles stolen
from the statues.
So many smiles.

The Tremor of Racehorses

Sometimes it's enough to put out the light
and sit
    in the night blue
    as the tremor of racehorses.
        But what if the tremor of racehorses is green?
        What if it's brown?

They said: Is yellow more red than white?
      Is a curtain more a table than
                         shoe?
      Is tobacco more pipe than
                        matches?

Really, stupid questions
and how they jeered.
      Only because they don't know
        the tremor of racehorses.
      That tremor of racehorses!

Rowanberries

                    Not that
we didn't expect it –
                    in the air
                    hung the scent of orange rowanberries,
                    circles that kept spreading out
                    until they were lost in infinity,
               and by small impatient
                                   motions of the hand
               we drove forward
                             place and time –
                                        we never
                                        knew anything
                                        better.

And someone said: It ought to be
                    rather a home, where space
                    kills the day,
                    ivy is God's love
                    and your eyes
                             have nowhere to go.

How we never
liked metaphors!
          A 'home', but where for God's sake
                    to go – in the rowanberries
                    no one could be misled.

          And so we dusted off
                             the statues of old saints,
          tried to define culture
          and went to bed,
               no worse
               than the distrustful
               with their perpetual smiles, who,
               we think, are their own
                         'ivy homes'...

Here, in this library,
where power and order
float like friends
among yellowing pages,
        we don't think too well
                    of ourselves –
                    But that we are better
                            than what came after
                    will be our cross.

The Stones Speak Czech

The stones speak Czech.
Water speaks salt
and remembers the salt
                    mines of the Mayas.
The clouds stand
like holes into some other country
that everyone remembers.
Only the Czechs do not remember.
Once they looked round their land
and were saddened
and became stones
which now speak Czech.
Take them in your hand
and go to sleep with them.
On this earth
not one Czech is left
but in a moment everyone
will be speaking Czech.

15/11/89

II

Black Tiger

Sometimes
there is only the black tiger
and the river with floating ashtrays.

Then
you throw away everything,
even yourself, gladly,
and you become
the black tiger on the floating
                              ashtrays.

You don't know why
nor what the black tiger and the river with the ashtrays
mean,

but it's a different ignorance
from
the constant fiddle with eternity,
from the black bottle of love,
god knows what's in it and
drink, man!

And the point is
that the tiger
comes only once.
Yes and you look for him
always and everywhere,
          in black hair
          in black eyes
          in black watches,

until suddenly
someone comes with candles
and then you are
again the black tiger,
only for a moment, so that at best
you can run away
and have eternity
stroke your chin
and say:
          You black tiger.

Jasmine Wind

Long we hauled
the jasmine wind
and the meaningless night
like books with a happy ending.

But when all the trucks
    the records of good intentions
    the hair of the gods
    last love's thimble
    and the football stadiums
    were not enough
we gave it up

and went for yeast beer
    to the pub beyond the bridge
light as a string that's just
    snapped
        and yet

someone was playing a song about a wedding
    and the wedding-cake
    whose sweetness
we cannot understand.

18/1/85

I can't move my head. That must be a window
in front of me,
            filtered and white. The sky
is full of white horses,
packed close together,
            you can't tell one from another. At times
black divisions
appear among them. Then
            we uncover a skull and quietly,
            unutterably, the seam of night
            splits. Alongside
it's you perhaps. You're full of jelly-bears,
you have them everywhere,
            they fall off and listen...
You'll rule them, those pale elves. You are
            an elf-king, troll
            with forgotten eyes.
    I don't know why I ask
    whether some day
            you'll write a poem about me.

Lovers in the Sand

They don't heed the sun. Like crabs, rather
jellyfish, these lovers in the sand,
gelatinous and white-hot.
                And as they strain after
                each other,
        because of the sand, because of the sand,
there are openings between their fingers through which life
escapes. Catch it!

        What do breasts mean –
        breasts and sand, a breast full of sand
                bursts,
        no more a baby's rattle. The sun has set
and the sand is cold. Before they change into corpses
the bodies rise
and go to a bistro
        for a slice of solid meat
        and solid bread.
    The bread disappears in the mouth,
    the jellyfish dies in the sand.

Tiredness

To go on kissing the soul, go on kissing the body, go on kissing heaven
until nothing's left,
>   only a necklace of melon seeds,
>   only tiredness rubbed with rosin,
>   tiredness like a big dog
>   covered with tar and feathers
>   that has pups ten times a day,
>   big dogs tarred and feathered.

But we didn't want that
we didn't think of that
and we didn't live that,
>   sighs last longer than screams,
>   screams turn run-down wheels in the air,
>   wheels that change into God's scooter,
but even it won't run over
a big tarred and feathered dog.

To go on kissing someone's soul, go on kissing someone's heaven
>   and then to rain sand
>   and snow ashes
>   and enjoy a blind man's holiday,
>   suicides fall from the windows
>   at the feet of small boys
>   and then not even that,
>   rosin   big dog   sighs screams   ashes
>   and then not even that.

One Prague Year

So many reproaches   So many scruples
        Old ladies with dogs and grey chignons
        stroll along the embankment
        Who knows how we'll end up

    and everything went badly –
    a college room and your scorched soul   I still
                        don't know what to call you
    nature stood stripped of sense
    and next door in the canteen they had draught beer
    you came to me for bread   books   a cigar
        your unsad sadness   your unexpecting
                        anything vital
        that point in your past where
        you cracked and now you swing on it
        like on a liana
    everything's otherwise   stupid intellectuals
    best to go and see a Belmondo where the world's in order
        brawls and lovely dolls   guns   the Amazon
        that's how it should be you said   just like that
        you were so scared of leaving yourself behind with someone
        and then having to go and visit yourself
        everywhere the beer's flowing and everyone
        chain-smokes and goes to see Belmondo
        smoking   drinking   gaping at Belmondo

Who knows how we ended up

Without Men

The women were glum
and like a tongue in hot wine

somewhere an axe was splitting wood
        it's not enough to look for a cock
                                at dawn
        even all the cats
        went to the cemetery that night

And the women drank
        as if long-haired boys
                                were asleep in the wine
        long-haired boys who revive
                        only in the mouth

Really, said one woman,
it's like in the war:
        no men

And they looked round
        laughing
        Yes certainly there's war they cried
        must be war
        otherwise they'd be sure to come
        otherwise they'd come

And why not, said Eve

And why not, said Eve
        and the serpent smiled
It has to be, God did not say as He watched Christopher Robin
        not tying his shoe laces

Do you smoke? said Man with brazenly long ears
and you accepted   why not
        the corpse on the motorway was cold
        and had green eyes

Not quite that, said Cain
           and he was sad
Do you smoke? said
        Man in a coat with a dark blue collar
and you accepted   why not
        They asked: And this is
           life, this emptiness
           of common blood, of common
           clay underfoot?

Who Knows Anything about Women?

Above you hang
majestic idols,
don't trust them, they are deserters
  from Fortune's wheel and never
  were beautiful,

a girl
in an ivory-white dress
is waving to you, her fingers
are copper
thimbles of the weird sisters,
    Put a log
    under Fate's cauldron
    and warm a finger,

the cooked idols
fall into the thimbles
and the girl is faceless, a desolate
west wind,
   it has worn away trees, towers, stones
   and eaten up the grass; some protruding bits
were left for the weeping
survivors; that's why
I lost you,
so that the west wind
would eat me up and the cooked idols
gobble my gentle friends,
    who have never known
    anything about women?

Go and say a prayer for me, sister

Go and say a prayer for me, sister,
voider
of my blood, final
blindness, with your ivy body and face of a page,
assurance drained
of destination, about whom I know nothing,
go and say a prayer for me, sister,
your comely pointed breasts,
your smoking silent all day in an easy chair,
your eyes are a northern sky in rain,
and hesitant, serene music
is the aura enfolding you
before which
I lean back my face,
you are end and presence without contours.

Voider
of my blood,
go and say a prayer for me
and don't ask
when I'll go and say a prayer for you.

We wanted to be silent
(for Petra)

We wanted to be silent, silent, silent,
                    no noisy
        vegetable patches, Wycliffian flow of talk,
        andante, adagio, love and death
                              on an old piano,
we wanted to be silent
              and not think of our breasts, hair and sex,

but angels halted above us
suspiciously and sniffed something strange,
six young actors passed by the fence
              and scented a lap,

we wanted to be silent but an old woman
                with a vegetable cart
        threw a couple of hundred kilo carrots at us and said
                            Good day.

The Gate of My Private Cemetery but Without Leopards

I won't have regrets, I won't love. Too well
combed leopards –

those happy endings. And little courage
to say that something is as it is, university

girls drinking coffee in the buffet
and thinking of the evening, of clean underwear.

Who will comb the leopards? They turned to me
and I said: I haven't a comb,

appropriate, quite appropriate.

Leopards' happy endings but the gate
of my private cemetery without leopards:
a thousand graves of mine, one of mother's

and one of yours, Petra.
If you bury your father
before you kill yourself in spirit...
Petra, you who once dreamt

of my hands.

New Year

At midnight when the bells
were ringing in the new year
I looked over my library
and at *The Perspectives of Man*
and then
at the redhead in Edvard Munch's 'Dance of Life' –
champagne and anchovies
in someone's flat.

When I woke up
two days later
I said
      Light, Sea, Radiance,
and I should have jumped up and run along the sand
into the wild waters of the sea.
On a long day
         to run leaves and sand through the fingers
         and enter a convent,
a purple convent
full of black sisters,
who would say to me:
         Sister, soon it will be
         Passion Week.

The year begins and brings
what the sea brings:
seaweed and dirt and splendid ships
with cheerful engines
and sails in love with the wind.

Get up, your eyes
         are nymphs' gems,
     your mouth Czech garnets,
     your body
         is in the care of the bird Roc
     that watches over
     sailors in the darkness.

Deep into the Body

Deep into the body
our gestures move away
deep into the sun
our eyes are lowered
       and smooth bare brows
       rest on our palms. Silence,
the silence of a leafless tree by the railway bridge.
       Such clear
brush strokes, luminous colours
on the background of heaven.

III

Self

Hands
   are here,
         mine,
but I'll get up and find
         their shape
imprinted on the window,
         a quiet hungry breathing out
         as of a deserted stone from the
                  Maya pyramids.
         What is left?
Beside a raven on the snow
I'll find my eyes
and further,
         on the last cliff
         of the North Sea
                  the sea murmurs and says:
                  I don't belong to myself,
                  I don't belong to myself.
In the end I'll see myself
naked amidst the monsters and lions
in the church of Nava del Rey or in Valladolid
                  or somewhere,
         on a chill morning
         that cripples the hands.

         Something here is always escaping,
         something is always missing
         and you're never whole,
                  within yourself
                  and alone, your words,
                           your breath
                  in the clouds of an alien sky.

Large Mirrors

I

And we spoke
of possible worlds, and
        occasionally
        he had an eye
            for the girls
   and she
   got up and left. My friend,
        who looked
        like the flag of Sweden.
   And 'the last of the Celts' left too,
        while he,
        the clever Jew,
        began to call me
            Arthur.
My friends.

II

        Plans for the future
        and large mirrors.
        Journeys, by train to the sunlit
           regions, a dream-book.
As dusk falls
the picture changes: an armchair,
        an old woman, me,
        drinking wine,
   the circles of good and the circles of evil
   are superimposed, interweave
        and disappear, the geometry
           of possible worlds,
   and where are they,
        my friends who gave me
           the large mirrors?
        An old woman
        in an old armchair
        as dusk is falling
           and the magic lines of the Kabbala
           and the lines on the brow
     are one and the same –

shan't I know what I really wanted,
        as I do now? There is always
        that blurred disillusion
        and the red dance of death
        in just one of possible worlds,
                quicker and quicker,

        a wax doll, an old woman
            in an old armchair
        in that best
        of all worlds...

From Hospital

I wake up at midnight
and like Cerberus
roam the endless corridors
on the look-out for something. White health?
Red roses on the tables
that drink up blood and memory?
Thoughts slide along the tiles
and I fail
to change them into memories.
There's nothing here to take hold of.
For the fifth day I've been thinking of my father,
of our walk along a dusty road
till we reached the edge of the forest.
There it ended.
I don't know what was in the forest.
I don't know when he died
or where I was at the time.
From morning to night
I eat my body,
drink my blood
and listen to my ears.
Like an animal
I guzzle my minutes
but can't get through them.

Perhaps I can be a madonna,
to be something,
something good that would take a granny
to the lavatory and pour tea
for a deaf old man?

The teapot has ugly blue flowers
and brings the afternoon nap
when I always die again.
For the first time I read Proust.
There exists only white, white.
Nothing of this is me.

The Death Mask

And I remembered Matthias Braun
    and his heavy flowing statues
        with open mouths,
  as if they wanted to grab everything within reach,
        Jesus ugly on the cross
        mouth open,
        little angels with forty-year-old imbecile faces
        mouths open,

and I remembered the death mask
        of my father
  looking like a beautiful woman,
        like the Unknown from the Seine,
  perhaps because they have
        the same whiteness
        and empty eyes without pupils
        and both are dead,

and I remembered an evening at the end of February
  when you asked if I could excuse your still being alive
        (on the table was a photo of Nezval with Picasso
        – Picasso just reached above his waist –
        united by art and camera)

and I remembered a house
        in Strossmayer Square
  where on the wall someone had written I Love You
        in white chalk,
  I Love You addressed to all passers-by,
  I go there when I feel I want to quit
  and have a death mask like a handsome man,
        like the Unknown from the Vltava,

I go there because that I Love You
        is the only one that lasts,
I stand with mouth
        wide open,
        lean my back on the tobacconist's stall
        and gaze at the chalk white
        as my father's death mask.

Touch of Death

The touch of death but first
bottomless black fire
                    at the feet, then
a chill breeze
from the depths of the bones
                    and a rattle
                    ruffling
the white air –
                    it could also have been
                    the yellow hands we gently
                    folded on the breast,
that gust
     without a word
     without a thought,
                    if you turned
                    your head,
                    it would rasp and fall apart.

The Unfinished Weight of the World

At times we catch the music of bones
      like the death of a beloved face
and lightly rub our eyelids,
      as if brushing away a night-moth
          or inert languor
          we can't get rid of.
Yet I wish I knew how
to walk among white beeches aware
that it all depends on me,
      that moment
      under the lonely skies.
That the Bible's message is
      Do what you can, man,
      for what I have created is good.

    And then again
    the music comes,
    the singing bones of vanity,
    which divert
    my soul
      beyond the horizon,
      beyond that taut string
      for which Anything
      is just Everything.
    There I stand inert
    empty-eyed
      inhuman
      like all who come to a place
      where you cannot weep.

    And only there
    I hear the crunching of fish spines
      deep in the mouth,
    the unfinished weight of the world.

And They Are Coming, the Guests Waiting for the Liquor

I saw my mother
    watering for the thousandth time
    a dead ibiscus,
I heard the libraries
        moaning
    when I read
    my father's memoirs
    and further on
    the night expresses
        drummed the rails –

and this is life, for this
you do everything,
for these moments
        of pure love?
        of sad love,
        for the moments of death,
when the implacable night-moths of radiance
bury the lamp
and resurrect the dead
        and they are coming –
        the guests waiting for the liquor,
        with their cheerful scepticism
          and colourful
          stories of the Lord
        they'll people again
        the rearranged house.

I still see today
the morning my father died
    and how far away
    the adults were,
    their world of shared signs,
    the politics and the coffee,
        far away –

and now I'm sitting here and waiting for the guests
in the rearranged house.
Shadows of the hired mourners laugh and call:
>Sylva!
>Come into the pit
>of offered mouths!
They are the maddened Furies
in black silk scarves, memory itself,
>who know nothing
>about death.

And they are coming, the guests waiting for the liquor...

Swans Smile just as Mechanically

I

Then you'll see me
as I tie the ribbons and make the wreaths, outdoing
    the chequeredness of the public word.

           And then I'll see you
painting the slogans, carefully
tinting the letters, as the colours shine
          in the communal sun. Then I'll see you
putting things and words
in order, a white full moon
    in a white sky:
            swans smile
            just as mechanically,
            melt and wilt.

II

          Ten lost sons
          are returning home, it's the ninth month,
            in the air headless dragons
            blossom and fade –

why was I
given these words, these smiles,
      the craven mouth of the cathedrals and
      he and she under a plane tree
      and 'the two thoughts that will save mankind',
      'the poor peasant smelling a flower
                t the wayside',
    all the stupid
    requisites of the world, the air stands still
            leaning on someone's arm, and
                  it hurts,
    its colourless crystals
fill the open graves, but that's
not the way, the world
        is there behind the window
        and how about
        that wardrobe.

Making Tea

How soothing it is, how things return
to their proper places,
                    and I think
                    of the Irish monks
                    and their unimagined ornaments
                    somewhere in history's depths.
The hand that pours the tea
can do no wrong: have some more,
        boy,
        more,
it'll be a long hard day, but you mustn't
be afraid of anything.

                    The Irish monk
                    inside the ornament
                    turns his head
                    and rips his hands
                              on lions' tails.
                    Have some more, boy,
                    more,
                    it'll be a long hard day,
                    there's that sweet prison
                    we promised you,
                    which you built yourself, boy.

The tea fills the cup,
the monk turns his head,
all the bloody
                    bits of flesh
                    will again become my hands.

When They Return to Holy Troy

They will have everything:
smiles and flowers and women,

they will bring long afternoons
                for the hands on the faces,
when the unicorns in the eyes
                raise
their fearful horn
in the green and white landscape
and the small birds
turn round and say, Yes?

The young sea
is a young god
without lotuses and sacrificial flesh,
                a powerful breath
                shaped and caressed by the smoke
from the bones of the sacrificial animals,
only a moment ago
their ox's heads waved
to the unicorn's white horn
and asked, Is it a god?

Luminous hands
bath the sea
like a small child,
the tiny sea folds itself
in a fish's eye, darkness
                last love
                through the eyelids –

That One Melody

The nation's traitor
sat on the eaves and sang,
the brass band in the courtyard
clapped till their fingers froze
and a man in uniform, the gravedigger,
handed round Chinese lanterns and tea.
    The creation of cathedrals.

And then the voices: Say, whom are you afraid of,
            what do you regret? Out with it,
    yes, that was what she wanted, that one
melody, one body,
    that one home, yes that's what
    she wanted, the song
        I composed for her, her song, otherwise
        she couldn't live.

And I'm sorry about everything, he said,
the evening
lies down at my feet
like an animal
and purrs. He has very fine
fur.

    You are barren country.
    You are your eyes, their tears tell lies.
    Your eyes you see always.

        – and she created cathedrals
            and said, I must stretch out
            on a light blue sea,
            please bring me fallen leaves
            to put under my soul.

Midnight Tea Drinker

I cut the bread and buttered a couple of slices.
I poured tea into two cups and began to drink.
Some elemental doings beyond the window scared me for a moment,
        but like Stilton cheese
        from a distance the drama
        drew near.
The first faded tulip petal fell into the fold of skin
        round my elbow and I felt
        I was getting old.
The tea was cold and I tried without luck
        to prompt the bread.
        No strength at all:
        couldn't lift the cup.
     I lowered my lips
     to its brim and saw
     the fly that had been looking me in the eye
     all the time.

The Only Place

I always stroked
my face with a violin bow
and my breast with the bow, I ate the horsehair
and became the empty space
inside the violin; I lie there
with a dead child
that cries. I don't cry. I could be

something like amber, but
immaterial, or air
        deep under the mountain
        where that aged Chinese
        caught sight of five suns; but next day
        there was only one.

Amber, I said, but only
its gold translucency,
the colour of the sea that in the morning
cries
under one sun
and one violin. The dead child
cries; it knows there's
only one sea. There
        we found ourselves:
naked, on a long
solitary beach,
        the only place
        where we shall ever belong.

The Bowler

The man in a bowler standing at the street corner
was so different from all those around him,
hurrying somewhere
or waiting for someone,
he wasn't waiting, he stood
maybe for the pleasure of standing,
very serious in his black bowler,
        as if he'd discovered some great truth,
        why the heart bleeds
        or what beauty is
        or how chimneys sleep,
        something just as trivial and useless,

he stood motionless,
but when a beautiful young leopard ran by,
the man slowly stretched out his hand
and in it the leopard hid its yellow
woman's eyes.

The Theory of Art

Scarlett O'Hara
had green eyes
and Rhett Butler an emperor's profile
on a Roman coin,
    decadent and cruel.

Voltaire drank twelve to fifteen
cups of coffee a day
and Andrew Bolkonski
saw heaven once.

And so on the fifth of June
nineteen eighty-seven
on a Leningrad street
I really met
young Raskolnikov: he was smoking a *belomorka*
    and went off once again
    to kill the old woman.

Because there isn't
one sea for the Flying Dutchman
and another for Columbus's galleons:
    the water they cross
    has the same sad salt.
    The sailors' waking eyes
    are full of women
        for ever.

I'm holding Ahasuerus
by the hand, Ahasuerus
kisses my cheek and all
    art theory
    reverts to the question:
    what became of
    Meresjev's legs?

Pax vobiscum

     Far on a beach
       some kind of solution
          at the mercy of the winds

Enter
that one man that one woman
all that is all that will be
And a child is crying
        in mid-ocean
All that was
  What do I have in my hand, sonny?
  Treasure, says the child
      and laughs
         into his father's empty palm

     And then you leave
     down the long alley
     in the foggy silence
     to the old mortuary,
        Pax vobiscum
     Forever alone
     and with a branch in hand   Your dog
     is scared of bells
        Was that all?
The child
reaches out his hand and says,
       I want it too
       I want it too
          the treasure

     Far on a beach
      always one solution
        at the mercy of the elements

The Primer

Not believe in love and love
not believe in death and die
dislike work and work

– Something else he said
something not everyone does

Believe in love and not love
believe in death and not die
like work and not work

– Something else please
something I haven't met with

Believe in love and love
believe in death and die
like work and work

– Yes that I wanted to hear he said quietly
When we sat at grandfather's dinner table
one chair was always left empty
in case the just Lord should pass by

And what is left, Scarlett

And what
is left, the lust for fate and 'My dear, how
     inconsistent you are', and green-eyed Scarlett O'Hara
     will say once again,
          I won't think of it now
          I'll think about it tomorrow

what
is left, the lights of the highway and
     home, only
          home,
     tell me whom you love best of all
     tell me, 'I missed you so much',
          coffee with whisky
          on an edgy morning,
     I won't think about it now

what will be left, Scarlett,
     a shadow cast
     like the memory of dust
          touched by my hands
          as it fell
          on my head
          instead of ashes,
     and so the air will keep
     the contours of a voice and a body, oh yes, Scarlett?
          They will say,
          'Yes, that was her,
          the motion, the light, the lie.'

Dark Potency

In you there was
a dark potency
you were like ginger
      and fish,
      ice cubes
      a dessert called 'Death by Chocolate',
eager to do good
implacable in offence

Like a priestess of white magic
you damned redemption and suicide
      and books
   with your voice of old reeds in a young wind
   with your starry tobacco eyes
      and passion for the fateful
in the end remained
      only sudden soothing
      touches of wind
      or
      'today a particularly ultramarine sky'
      and many long past perfumes
         that always brought
         tears

Silence

She needed so much to hear silence
complete silence
standing in the white fields
and in the soundless air a deep voice
slowly calling
her name

The Pripet Marshes

I thought of you
during my long train journey
to where the world ends. Where the fields lie listless,
        the flowers faded
        in puked colours.
Where the lungs are a cowshed, the land's
only life. And the warm straw may catch fire
        at any moment.

The dead mirror of the marshes reflected for me
a stranger's face; who was down there, who was burying
        treasure under the bog?

The reeds swayed and laughed
and my hand kneaded
the living mud, all the warm unburied
        dead.

        Above in the brown sky
        hung a heavy bell
        and its heart
        beat out the hidden
        deep under the bog
        and sounded the measure of the Lord.

Girl with a Hasidic Candle

He whistles, whistles,
the boy in the song
about a Hasidic candle
like me
a century ago
   when I would run
   across the abysmal Galician plain
   and dig up
   old Hasidic books
             on the edge of the cemetery.

The candle burns long
and brightly; in its flame
my eyes are held complete:
         I gaze into them
         as at pictures
         of past reincarnations,
         fly, saints, and someone's son,
he whistles, whistles,
the boy in the song
about a Hasidic candle
and his flame is joy.

Side-whiskered Jews are coming out of the synagogue
and a girl
   with a lit candle,
   who belongs nowhere,
walks in front of them
as in front of any
         procession in history,
         before any kind
of thought about joy, beauty, God and death.

Death that comes
with one eye
in the middle of the forehead
                    and with a Cyclopean candle
                    grasped in human
                    hands:
the wax-dripped fingers
smell like the sweet parchment skin
                    of the newly born.

Notes

'The Stones Speak Czech': The poem is dated as written just before 17 November 1989, which saw the beginning of the democratic revolution in Czechoslovakia.

'The Death Mask': Matthias Braun (1684-1738) was a famous Czech sculptor of Austrian origin. His many statues have an emotional intensity and distorted features reminiscent of Rome High Baroque. Vítězslav Nezval (1900-1958) was an outstanding Czech lyric poet and translator of modern French poetry. A well-known poem is 'Neznámá ze Seiny' (The Unknown Girl Taken from the Seine).

'The Theory of Art': *Belomorka* is a Russian cigarette. Meresjev is the hero of Boris Polevoj's Second World War novel, based on fact, *The Story of a Real Man*. After his plane crashed, he crawled to safety, had both legs amputated, was fitted with artificial limbs and continued as a pilot.

'The Pripet Marshes': A large expanse of often desolate marshland in the western part of the Soviet Union.

Biographical notes

Sylva Fischerová was born in Prague in 1963. She lived for twenty years in the Moravian town of Olomouc, where her father, a distinguished philosopher and sociologist, had been rector of Olomouc University. After 1948 his non-Marxist outlook prevented him from publishing in his own country. Fischerová studied philosophy and physics at Charles University, Prague, and is now completing a degree course in Greek and Latin.

Her poems first appeared in two anthologies of young Czech poets in 1985, *Special Sign* (Zvláštní znamení) and *Germinating* (Klíčení). Her first collection, *The Tremor of Racehorses* (Chvění závodních koní), was published in 1986 by Mladá Fronta in Prague. Her second book, *Large Mirrors* (Velká zrcadla), is due out from Československý Spisovatel, Prague, in 1990.

She took part in the Child of Europe readings at the Royal Festival Hall, South Bank, London, in February 1989, and is featured in the *Child of Europe* anthology, edited by Michael March (Penguin Books, 1990). *The Tremor of Racehorses: Selected Poems*, translated by Jarmila and Ian Milner (Bloodaxe Books, 1990), is her first book to be published in English.

Jarmila Milner was born in Czechoslovakia in 1913. After graduating in English at Charles University, Prague, she had a postgraduate fellowship at Vassar and Columbia University, USA, and was a United Nations officer in New York and Prague from 1947 to 1958. Her husband, **Ian Milner**, was born in 1911. He is a New Zealander and an Oxford graduate, a UN officer (1947-51), and later professor of English literature at Charles University. They live in Prague.

They have translated Petr Bezruč (Artia, Prague, 1966), Vladimír Holan (*Selected Poems*, Penguin, 1971, and *A Night with Hamlet*, Oasis Books, 1980), Miroslav Holub (five books from Penguin, Jonathan Cape, Secker & Warburg, and Bloodaxe Books, three of these in collaboration), Sylva Fischerová (*The Tremor of Racehorses*, Bloodaxe Books, 1990), and Josef Hanzlík (*Selected Poems*, Bloodaxe Books, 1991, with Ewald Osers). Their versions of various modern Czech poets appear in the anthologies *The Poetry of Survival*, edited by Daniel Weissbort (Anvil Press and Penguin, 1990) and *Child of Europe*, edited by Michael March (Penguin, 1990). Their latest publication projects are an anthology of contemporary Czech poetry and an enlarged selection of Vladimír Holan's poetry.